Money Coun

MW00904154

Shirley Duke

rourkeeducationalmedia.com

Teacher Notes available at
rem4teachers.com

www.rourkeeducationalmedia.com

PHOTO CREDITS: Cover: © Dibrova, Design56, malerapaso; Title Page: © nautilus_shell_studios; Page 3: © arsgera, Vova Pomortzeff, George D.; Page 4: © Maartje van Caspel; Page 5: © Philip Dyer, jo unruh; Page 6, 8, 10, 11, 12, 13: © Vova Pomortzeff; Page 7: © Christophe Testi; Page 9: © Vova Pomortzeff, Christophe Testi; Page 14: © Cobalt88, Andy Dean; Page 15: © Cobalt88, Vova Pomortzeff; Page 16: © darko64 Vova Pomortzeff; Page 17: © Jose Manuel Gelpi Diaz; Page 18: © Andy Dean, Eric Ferguson; Page 19: © Vova Pomortzeff, Aleksandar Zoric; Page 20: © Aleksandar Zoric, Christophe Testi; Page 21: © Eric Ferguson, Vova Pomortzeff, Christophe Testi; Page 22: © Cobalt88, Andy Dean, Aleksandar Zoric, Vova Pomortzeff; Page 23: © Cobalt88, Vova Pomortzeff;

Edited by Precious McKenzie

Cover design by Teri Intzegian
Interior design by Renee Brady

Library of Congress PCN Data

Money Counts / Shirley Duke
(Little World Math)
ISBN 978-1-61810-076-4 (hard cover)(alk. paper)
ISBN 978-1-61810-209-6 (soft cover)
Library of Congress Control Number: 2011944386

Rourke Educational Media
Printed in the United States of America,
North Mankato, Minnesota

Educational Media

rourkeeducationalmedia.com
customerservice@rourkeeducationalmedia.com • PO Box 643328 Vero Beach, Florida 32964

Money means coins and bills.

Work earns money.

You buy things with money.

 means cent

$ means dollar

Each kind of money has a name.

penny

nickel

dime

quarter

half dollar

dollar

One penny = 1¢

One nickel = 5¢

One dime = 10¢

One quarter = 25¢

One half dollar = 50¢

One dollar = 100¢

Can you make 5¢?

pennies   or   nickel

Now, can you make 10¢?

10 pennies

or

5 pennies and 1 nickel

or

2 nickels

or

1 dime

How much money do you have?

+ = 10¢

+ = 25¢

+ = 25¢

Can you make one dollar with coins?

10 dimes

or

4 quarters

or

2 half dollars

How many pennies equal $1.00?
How many nickels equal $1.00?

How much for two candies?

5¢
each

15

I have a quarter.
That's too much!

You get change.

25 cents − 10 cents = 15 cents.

17

I'll buy a toy. Is this enough?

75¢
each

That is 25¢.
You need
more money.

This is more than enough!
I will get change!

 – 75¢ =

1 quarter
in change

75¢

What can I buy with my change?

5¢ each

YUM!

5¢ + 5¢ + 5¢ + 5¢ + 5¢ = 25¢

Index

Websites

www.usmint.gov/kids/games/dollarDive/

www.mathworksheetwizard.com/grade1/grade1money.html

www.superteacherworksheets.com/countingmoney/
    count-money-mixed-coins.pdf

About the Author

Shirley Duke likes writing about money. She likes to spend it, too. She lives and shops in Texas and she always counts her change.

Ask The Author!
www.rem4students.com